Art Director Charles Matheson
Art Editor Ben White
Editor James McCarter
Illustrators Chris Forsey
Hayward Art Group
Jim Robins

Designed and produced by
Aladdin Books Ltd
70 Old Compton Street
London W1

First published in
the United States in 1984 by
Franklin Watts
387 Park Avenue South
New York, NY 10016

Library of Congress
Catalog Card No: 83-51329

ISBN 531-04743-1

Printed in Belgium

Franklin Watts Science World

Biology

Ifor Evans

Series Editor: Lionel Bender

FRANKLIN WATTS
New York · London · Toronto · Sydney

Introduction

Biology is the science of living things. It studies what makes them alive, how they feed and reproduce, and how all the millions of plants and animals in the world have come to be the way they are.

The great variety of life forms can be noticed in just a short walk in a city park: there are trees, grasses, birds, insects and mammals such as cats and dogs. A microscope shows us that all living things – including ourselves – are made of tiny units called cells. Cells are the building blocks of life, and are as important to biology as atoms are to chemistry.

Cells are themselves made of chemicals – the food we eat gives us a supply of chemicals that we need to make new cells for growth, or to repair damaged cells.

There is one chemical that is particularly important to living things. This is called DNA and is found in the cells of all living things. In the chapters on Reproduction and on Evolution we see how DNA enables offspring to have some characteristics from each of their parents, and how this can lead, over many generations, to plants and animals becoming better suited, or adapted, to the places where they live.

The final chapters of this book look at plants, animals and microbes in turn. All of these living things depend upon one another to survive – there is a balance in nature in which animals, plants and microbes are linked together. Life's diversity and the complex relationships between living things make biology one of the most fascinating of the sciences.

Living things can be seen everywhere, even in a handful of garden soil or a jar of pond water. One of the things common to all living things is that they grow and have offspring. Although they seem at first sight very different, most plants and animals reproduce in fundamentally the same way: the true difference between them lies in the way they obtain the food they need. One of the most important aspects of biology – *ecology* – studies the way in which the plants and animals of the living world are dependent on each other for their survival.

Looking at living things.

Growth and reproductio

Contents

Plants and animals

Ecology

Diversity

Our planet is a living world, full of extraordinary and beautiful life forms or "organisms." You can discover this diversity for yourself without visiting a natural history museum or zoo. Spend some time in your local park or perhaps picnic by a stream in summer – and look around you. You will see living things everywhere – in the air, on the ground and in the water.

The biologists' name for a group of similar individual organisms is a "species." For example, all the gray squirrels in the world are of the same species. They are able to breed among themselves, but not with animals from another group. A squirrel and a rat are obviously different species that will never breed together. Some species, however, are much more alike. Gray and red squirrels differ only in minor features such as fur color and ear tufts, but they are unable to breed together and so are considered to be two different species.

There are over two million different species of plants and animals on Earth and new species are being discovered all the time. Biologists have sorted out many of the species, by putting all those with similar features – squirrels and chipmunks, for example – into the same group. These groups are made into even larger groups, until we reach the five largest groups, called the kingdoms. This sorting process is called classification, and helps biologists to understand the relationships among the multitude of plants and animals.

Naming species
Many species have ordinary names, but this name might be used for different animals in different countries. So each species is given a unique scientific Latin name, used by all biologists. Human beings are *Homo sapiens* which means "man, wise."

▷ There is a wealth of species to be found in woods and by the riverbank during the summer. Plants are at the peak of their growing period and many birds, animals and insects are active. Another reason for the large number of species is the varied nature of their surroundings. Here, we can see at least three kinds of home, or habitat, in which the plants and animals are living. There is a grassy meadow, a freshwater stream and a woodland edge. Each of these habitats has its own characteristic species.

▽ A quiet riverside in the summer is a good place to see many different kinds of animals and plants. Brightly colored flowers and insects catch the eye. Butterflies look for places to lay their eggs. Birds are busy seeking food for their young broods. You can catch tadpoles, fish and water beetles to study – but put them back afterward.

What Makes Something Alive?

Feeding, growing and reproducing

All living things feed, grow and reproduce. The caterpillar (1) feeds greedily and grows quickly. In the "pupa" stage (2), the insect's body changes rapidly to become a winged adult (3). The adult insects mate and the female lays eggs, from which young caterpillars hatch out, so beginning the life cycle again.

The life cycle of a butterfly

Respiring and excreting

All organisms need energy for growth and movement. Animals respire or breathe to take in oxygen from the air, which is used to release energy from food. Waste products are excreted, for example by breathing out, sweating or urination. Plants respire, but they also combine carbon dioxide and water, using energy from the Sun, to make their food.

A racehorse sweating after a race

Sensing and moving

All organisms are aware of their surroundings and can react to them. For instance, a fly has various sense organs with which it sees, hears and smells. It has muscles that enable it to move by walking or flying. Although plants cannot see and have no muscles, they can detect light and grow towards it. The Venus flytrap plant can actually feel the flies which it traps within its special leaves.

A Venus flytrap plant

Grouping Living Things

A hamster's relatives

You don't need to be an expert to tell that this is a hamster, nor to guess that it is closely related to the guinea pig. Its next closest relatives are the squirrels and other rodents. These animals share many characteristics because they are descended from common ancestors. By classifying a hamster we can find some of its other relatives.

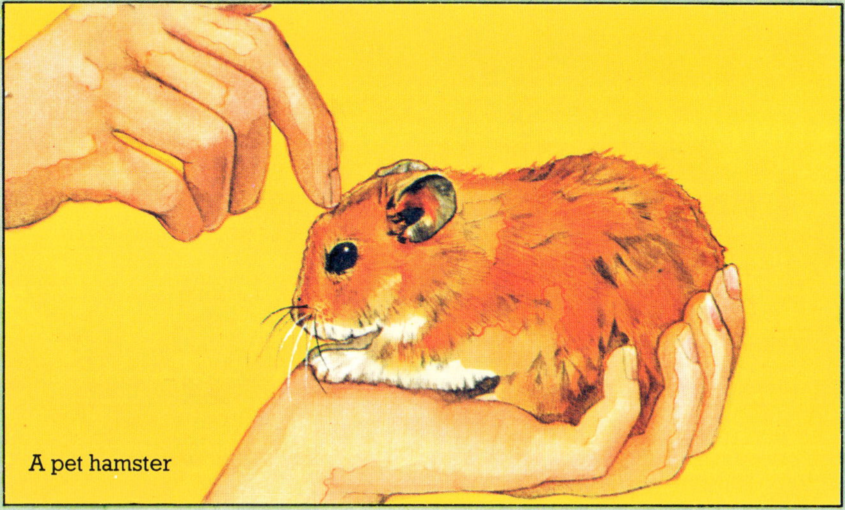

A pet hamster

The kingdoms of living things

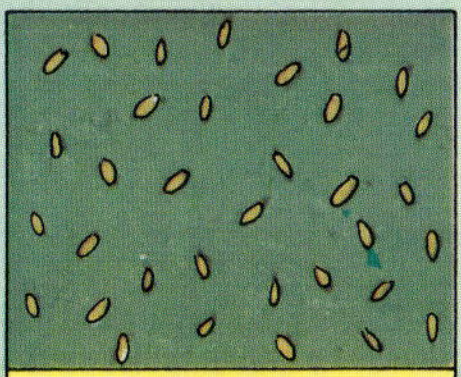

Monera

The simplest of all microscopic organisms, with a simple method of reproduction. The group includes bacteria and the blue-green algae.

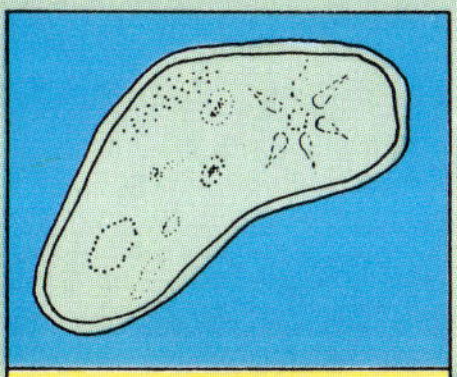

Protista

These are single-celled organisms. Most, like the Amœba, can only be seen with a microscope. Some can move about by changing their shape.

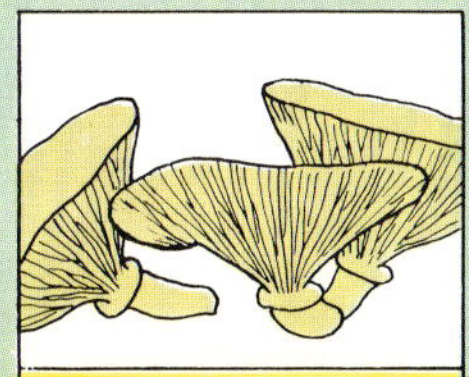

Fungi and Yeasts

Plants that feed on other organisms – living or dead. Some fungi are microscopic, but others, such as mushrooms, can grow quite large.

Higher Plants

Green plants ranging from mosses and ferns to flowering plants and trees. They can make their own food from simple chemicals by using the Sun's energy.

Higher Animals

A great variety of complex animals including worms, starfish, insects, reptiles, birds and human beings. They feed on plants or other animals.

Classifying a hamster

Like all living things the hamster belongs to one of the five kingdoms shown above. Firstly hamsters belong to the *order* of rodents. Rodents in turn belong to the *class* of mammals. Mammals are grouped with other animals that have backbones, such as birds, fish and reptiles. These go into a higher grouping called a *phylum*. Many phyla make up the *kingdom* of higher animals to which the hamster belongs.

Kingdom	Animals
Phylum	Chordates
Sub-phylum	Vertebrates
Class	Mammals
Order	Rodents
Species	Hamster

The Unifying Cell

A pond full of green, scummy water doesn't, at first sight, seem the best place to find out more about how living things work. But if you take a sample and look at it carefully, you'll probably find a few threads of pondweed and one or two water snails. You may also see tiny darting specks, the size of grains of sand, which are in fact minute animals, related to crabs and shrimps.

But these are not the only living creatures in your sample. A powerful microscope will reveal a world of even smaller, stranger creatures. Some are long and wormlike, others are round-bodied and covered with tiny hairlike filaments. They look as bizarre as anything dreamt up by science fiction filmmakers!

Many of these microscopic organisms have one thing in common – they consist of just one cell. A cell is the building block of life – it is the smallest unit of life that can exist on its own. All living things are made of cells, from the smallest insect to the largest mammal, from the simplest pondweed to the tallest tree.

Organisms made up of many cells – and most living things are made up of more than one cell – are called "multicellular." In multicellular organisms there are many different types of cells, each designed for different purposes. These cells build different organs, such as the brain or liver in mammals, or roots and leaves in plants. An organism can be thought of as similar to an assembled jigsaw – cells assembled together make organs, and the organs combine to make the complete individual plant or animal.

A jar of murky pond water may contain millions of microscopic life-forms. The slipper-shaped *Paramecium* uses the hairs on its body to move about. *Spirogyra* is a string of independent cells. The round-bodied organism is *Chlamydomonas*. *Euglena* is cucumber-shaped.

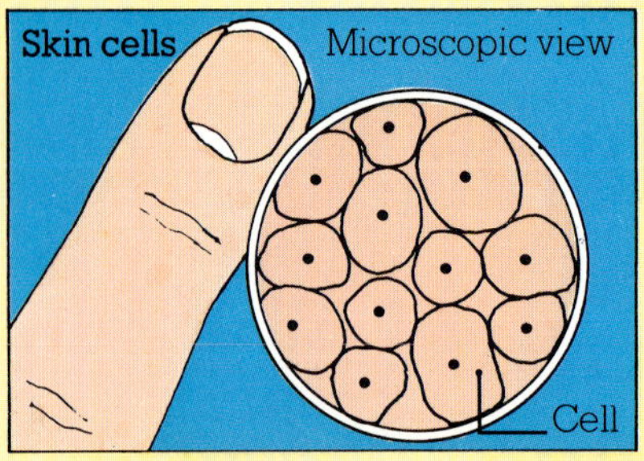

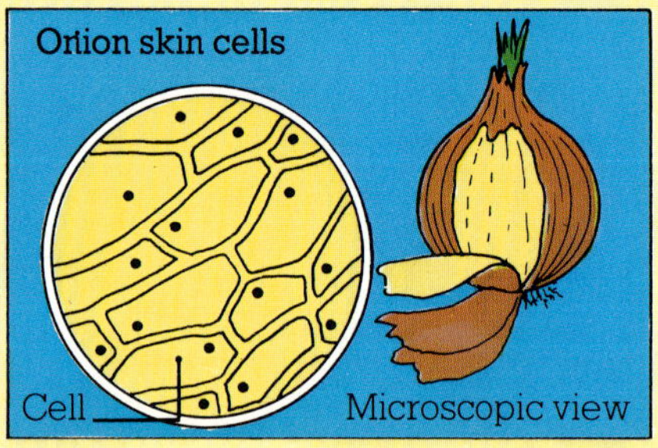

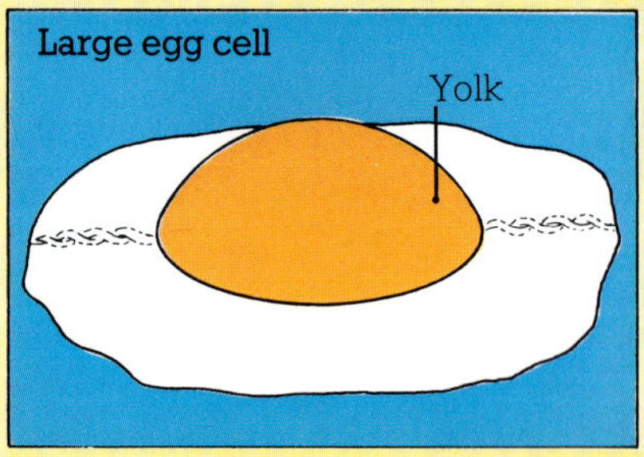

Looking at Cells
When you look at your skin, you are seeing a flat sheet of tough, protective cells, although each individual cell is too small to be seen with the naked eye. The thin, transparent skin you find between the layers of an onion is in fact just one cell thick. But not all cells are microscopic. A chicken's egg yolk is a huge, single cell. It contains enough food for the developing chick until it hatches out.

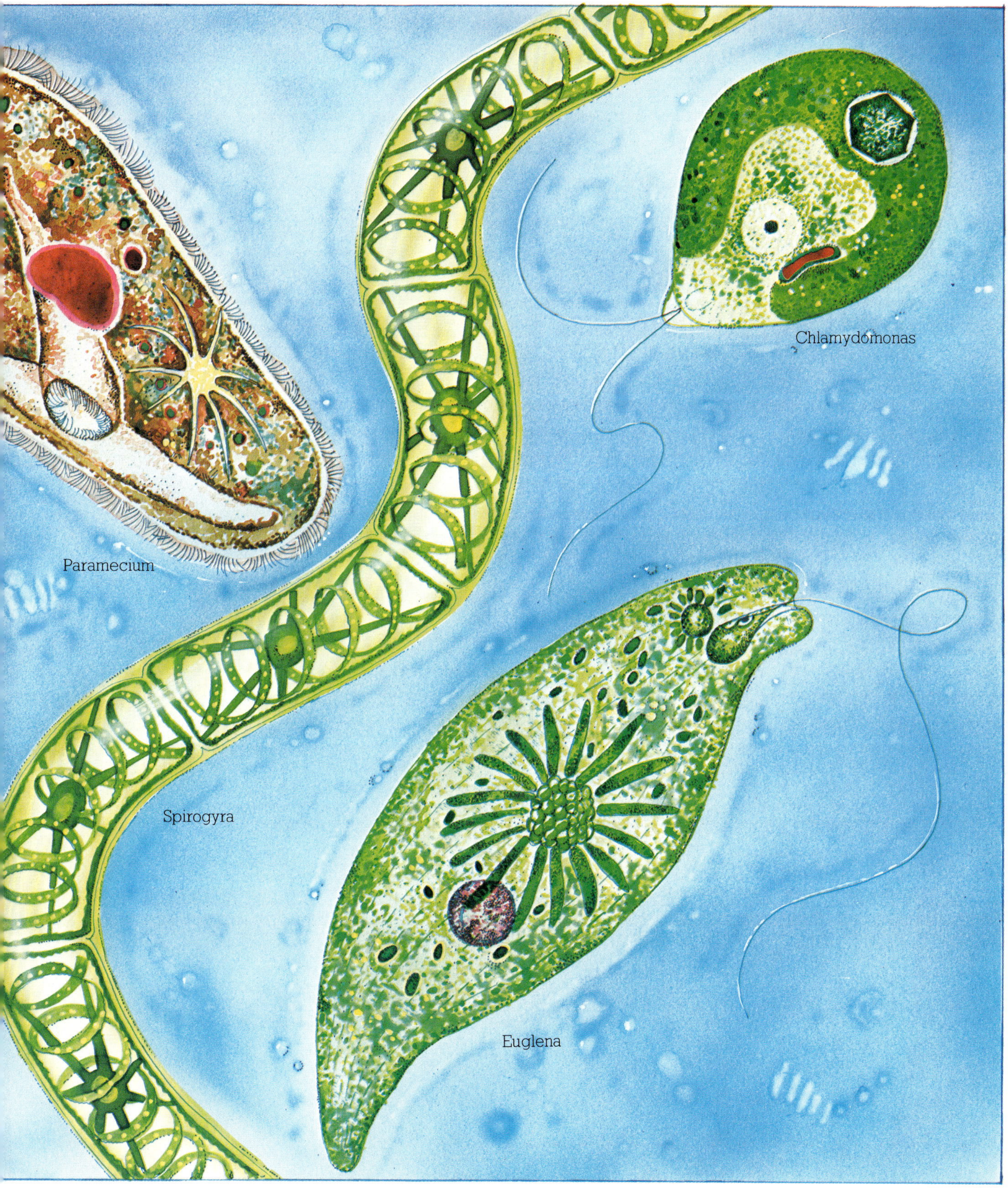
Paramecium
Chlamydomonas
Spirogyra
Euglena

Plant and Animal Cells

Both plants and animals are constructed of cells that look similar at first sight under the microscope. The cells of both are fluid-filled bags containing small specialized regions such as the nucleus. But there are a number of significant differences. Plant cells, for example, have a thick, rigid cell wall which is missing in animal cells. This is what makes plants firmer to the touch – compare the texture of a slug to a crisp young cabbage leaf and you'll see the difference that the cell wall makes! Highlighted below are the most important constituents that make up the structure of plant and animal cells.

Slugs feeding on a cabbage leaf

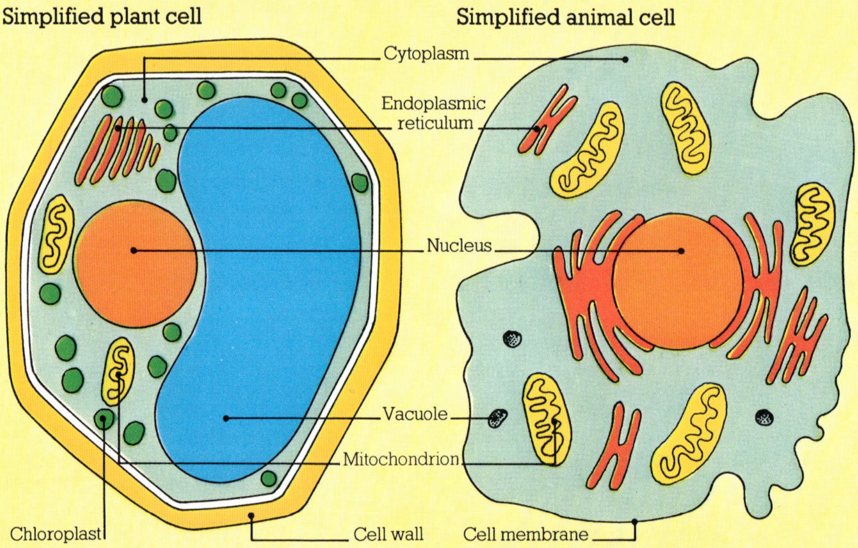

Nucleus

The nucleus is surrounded by a thin membrane (skin) and is often found in the center of the cell. It is the control center and directs the cell's activities.

Cytoplasm

The clear, watery fluid which makes up the bulk of the cell. In it are suspended all the internal parts of the cell, as well as complex chemicals which the cell makes or uses.

Vacuoles

These are fluid filled spaces suspended in the cytoplasm. Most plant cells have a single large vacuole that keeps the cell rigid. Animal cells often have several small vacuoles.

Cell Walls and Membranes

All cells are surrounded by a thin, flexible membrane. But the membranes around most plant cells have a protective cell wall, made of material called cellulose.

Endoplasmic Reticulum

This is a maze of tiny, hollow, interconnected tubes found throughout the cytoplasm. Biologists think these form a transportation system for chemicals within the cell.

Chloroplasts

These are found only in plant cells. They are disk-shaped structures packed with a green pigment called chlorophyll which helps the plant to make its food.

Mitochondria

These hollow sausage-shaped structures are found in all cells. Through a process called cell respiration they provide energy for all the cell's activities.

Building Bodies

Although all organisms are made up of cells, these cells are by no means all the same – the cells that make up our blood must obviously be different from those that make up the outer layer of our skin. In human beings, for example, red blood cells, that carry oxygen, have a relatively simple structure. Nerve cells, such as those found in the brain and spinal column, are much more complex. Muscle cells are particularly elastic – they can stretch and relax again, enabling us to move our limbs. All the different cells in an organism are not, of course, just thrown together in a confused heap. They are carefully arranged in special patterns to form definite structures, just as the bricks, timbers and tiles of a house are arranged to form the walls and roof.

Specialized human cells

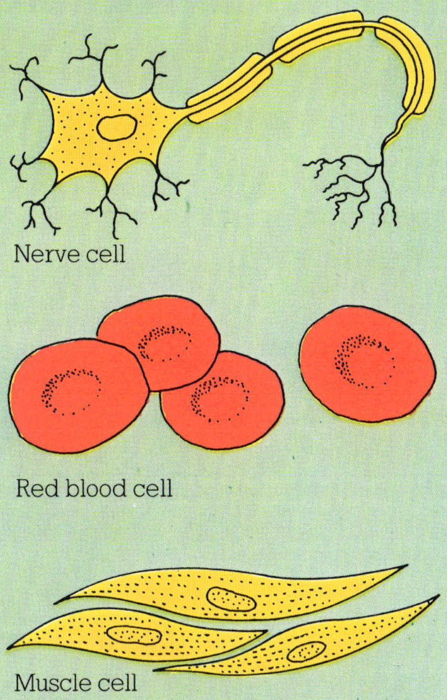

Cells specialized to do a specific task group together to form tissues. The lining of animal stomachs is an example of a tissue. Several different types of tissues make up organs – parts of plants and animals that have definite jobs, such as the heart or a plant's roots. Different organs work together in organ systems. The heart and lungs are part of the blood's circulatory system. Finally, all the organ systems combined form the complete organism.

An animal

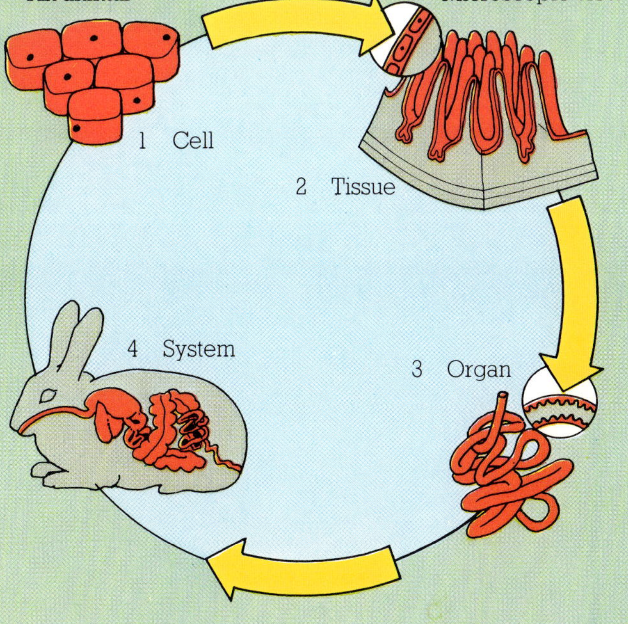

A plant

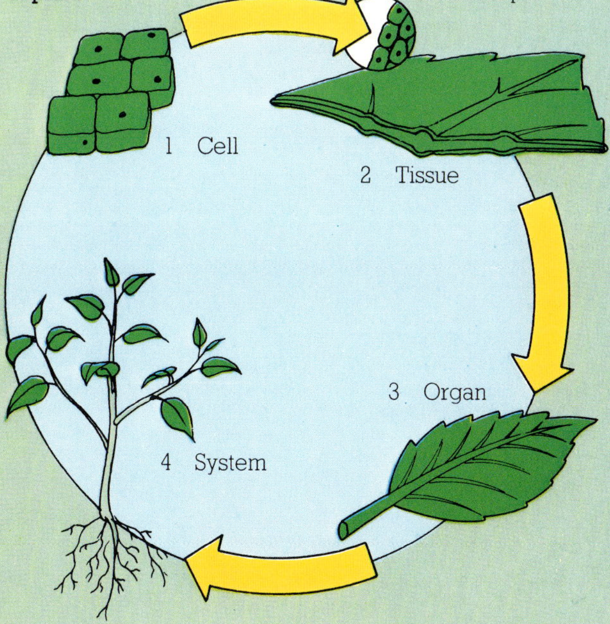

The Chemistry of Life

All living things are built up from cells; but what are the cells themselves made of? One of the main constituents of all cells – plant and animal – is water. The human body is about 70 percent water! Water is closely followed by carbon – the charred black lump of a burnt steak is the carbon remains of its cells. Carbon and the elements of water – hydrogen and oxygen – are chemicals, and from chemicals such as these, cells are built.

Chemicals by themselves are lifeless and it is only when they are brought together and correctly assembled that a living cell is produced. Because cells are so complex, many thousands of different chemicals are found within them. Chemicals that are found in living things are called "biochemicals."

The chemicals inside cells react with one another to produce different chemicals that the cell needs. Bees are a good example of such living "chemical factories." Inside their bodies, bees change the nectar of flowers to honey, a much thicker, sweeter substance than nectar.

Three main types of biochemicals are important in building cells – proteins, fats and carbohydrates. These are all familiar as part of our diet – we take them in as food to provide a chemical supply for the processes that take place in our bodies. But one other type of biochemical is especially important to living things. This is called DNA – short for deoxyribonucleic acid – and it controls the way new cells are made and old ones repaired. DNA is the chemical key to the way lifeless chemicals can create living cells, and to the way cells build up to become plants or animals.

△ A beekeeper removes a frame bearing a honeycomb from a hive. The comb is a series of six-sided wax chambers used to contain the honey. Bees produce and store honey as food for the young grubs that develop in the hive.

Chemical components
This is a "chemical recipe" for a human being. The bulk of it is made up of the two elements of water, and carbon, the element of coal. These three chemicals, and traces of others such as iron and magnesium, are combined to make the many different components, or biochemicals, from which cells and bodies are built.

▷ This beekeeper uses several biochemical materials in his daily work. He wears a cotton mask and his hives are wooden. Cotton comes from cotton plants, and all wood, an immensely versatile material, was originally the water – conducting and supporting tissue of trees. Rubber, too, is a biochemical substance. It is prepared from latex, a thick, white juice tapped from rubber trees.

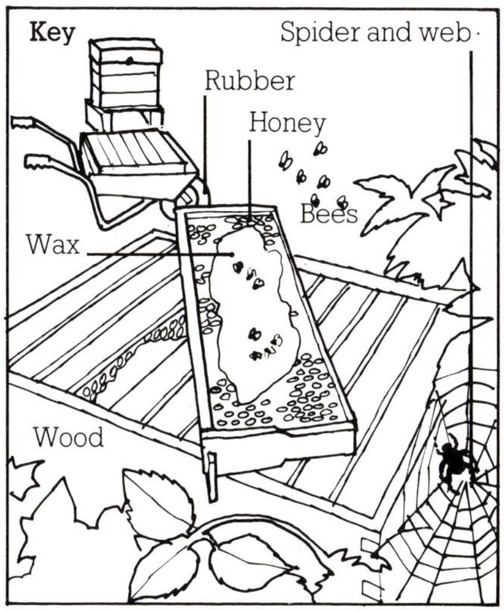

Biochemicals

Biochemicals are the non-living substances from which living cells are made. There are four main groups of biochemicals that are especially important in the life of a cell. Three of these, proteins, carbohydrates and fats are the cell's building blocks. The fourth group contains nucleic acids, and it is to this group that DNA belongs. DNA acts as the cell's information carrier. It is found in the cell's nucleus and controls such activities as repairing damaged cells and the production of new cells for growth.

Child's popper beads

Many biochemicals are built up from thousands of small units, each containing atoms of elements such as carbon, oxygen and hydrogen. Imagine a string of popper beads. Each bead can represent one of these small units. A large number of units in a biochemical, such as a protein or DNA, are linked together to form a chain, in the same way as the string of beads is made up.

A Chemical Code – DNA

The biochemical DNA is rather like a rope ladder that has been twisted into a spiral. The two halves of the ladder are made up of long chains of units called "nucleotides." The rungs of the ladder are made up of four units called "bases" – here shown as red, blue, green and yellow. The bases are in fact part of the nucleotides and are always found in the same pairs. In this example, red always pairs with blue, and green with yellow. The order of bases along the DNA forms a code that enables it to carry all the information needed to build new cells.

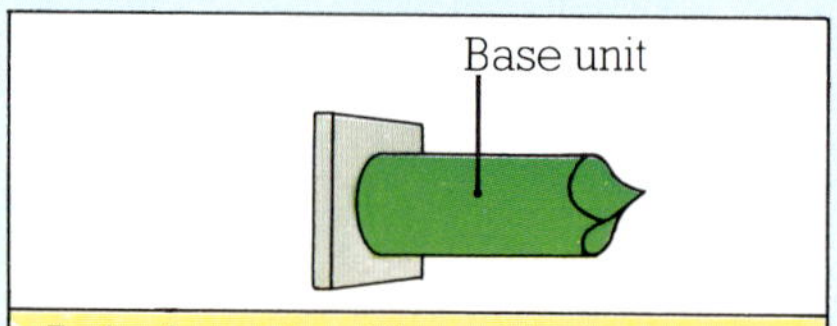

A single nucleotide and its base unit.

The four nucleotide bases.

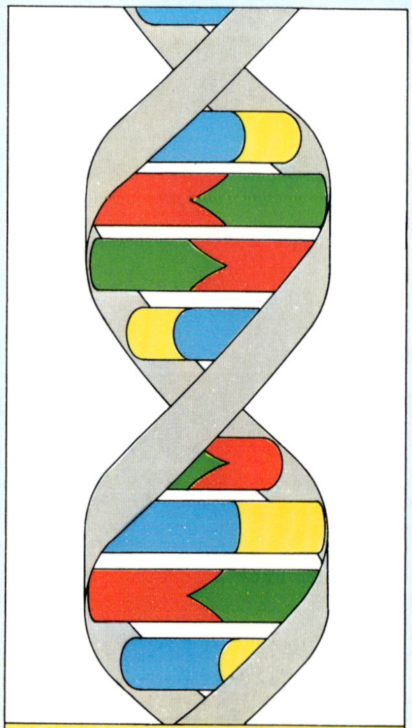
A short section of a DNA molecule.

Making Proteins

What is a protein?
Proteins are built up of chains of units called amino acids. There are many thousands of different proteins, each with a different sequence of amino acid units. This variety means that proteins can perform a vast number of functions in living creatures. For example, the proteins in skin make it tough and flexible. Some proteins digest food. Others help to make new cell materials.

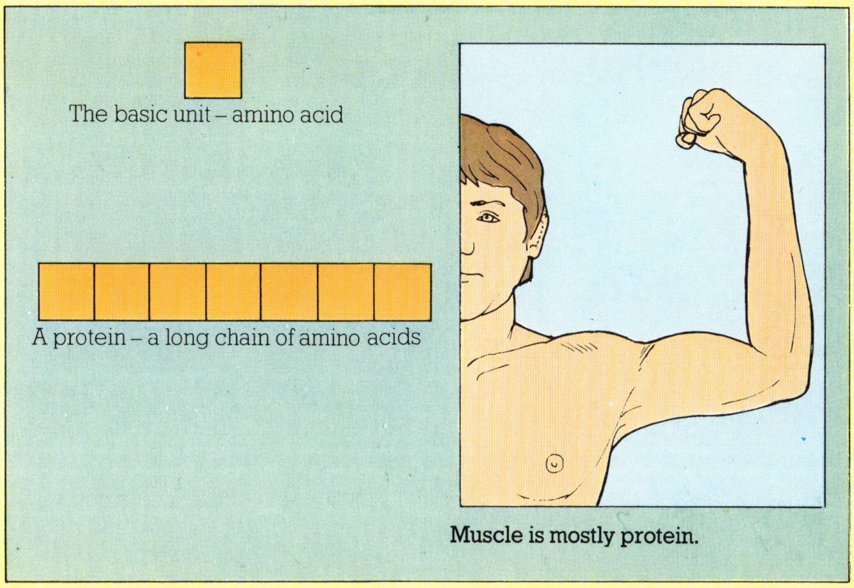

Muscle is mostly protein.

The DNA code and proteins
It is the order of amino acid units that gives a protein its special properties, making it perhaps a leaf, root, muscle or skin protein. Information stored in the DNA's chemical code is used to put the amino acid units into the correct order to make every kind of protein found in cells. Each amino acid is represented in the DNA code by its own special group of three base units. For example, red, blue, green maybe the code for one particular amino acid; blue, yellow, yellow for another and so on. If we take one strand of a DNA molecule, we can "read" its base units in groups of three. By following along the strand, we can read out the sequence of amino acids – and thus the protein – it produces. A section of a DNA molecule that has the complete code for a single protein is called a gene. DNA molecules are so long that they contain thousands of genes, each with its code for making a different protein. Proteins are used in cells to make new cell materials and are also the building blocks of cells themselves. The DNA, which is contained in the nucleus of each of our cells, stores enough information to build not just another cell, but also a complete human body!

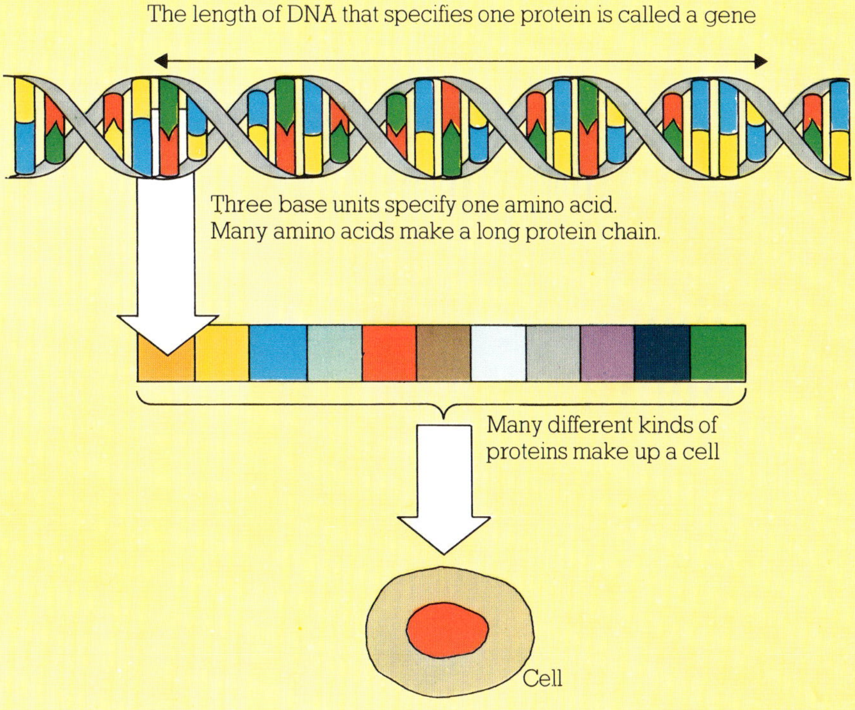

Reproduction, Growth and Heredity

One of the most important characteristics of living things is that they grow and are able to reproduce. Each spring new plants appear to replace those that died in winter and these new plants will in turn produce seeds from which the following year's stock will grow.

The offspring of a species is always the same species as its parent or parents – we wouldn't expect a cow to give birth to anything other than another cow! Similarly, we expect human offspring to be like their parents. We talk about children "inheriting" some of their parents' characteristics – a newly-born baby might be said to have its father's curly hair and its mother's blue eyes.

To understand how these characteristics are passed from one generation to the next, we must look at the way that living things reproduce. The simplest plants and animals, such as single-celled organisms we saw in pond water, simply split into two. Others grow a bud of cells from which an adult develops. But mammals, birds, reptiles, insects and many plants use a more complicated method known as sexual reproduction.

Genes and chromosomes

DNA is the code of life that enables living things to pass on their characteristics to their offspring. As we have seen, long strands of DNA are called genes. The genes themselves are linked together to form even longer strands called chromosomes. Chromosomes may contain many thousands of genes. They are found in the cell nucleus and usually occur in pairs. In human cells there are 23 pairs of chromosomes. When a cell simply divides the two new cells have identical chromosomes. In sexually reproducing organisms the offspring has some chromosomes from both parents.

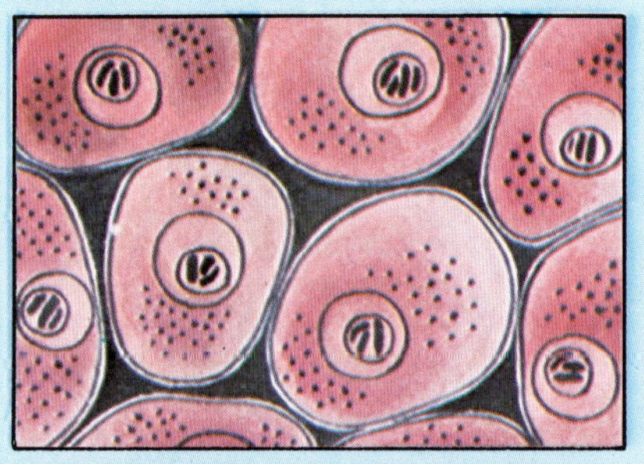

A group of cells

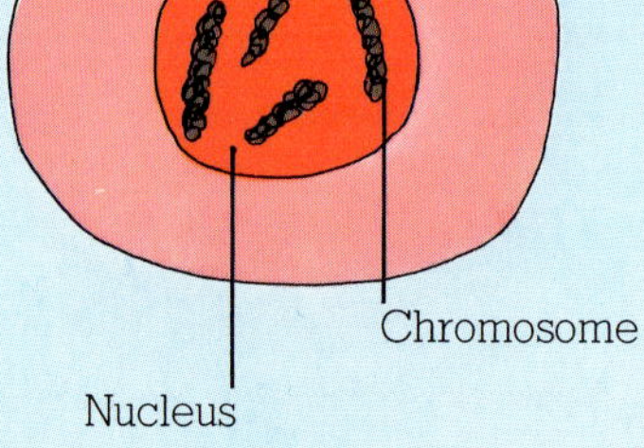

A single cell

▽ Farm animals such as cows inherit certain characteristics, such as hair color, from their parents. These characteristics vary among different offspring of the same parents.

In sexually-reproducing plants and animals there are two special cells – the sex cells – involved in producing offspring. Sometimes these cells are made by the same organism but more usually they are produced by separate male and female individuals. Male sex cells are called sperms and female sex cells are eggs. When a single sperm fuses with, or "fertilizes," a single egg cell, a new cell is produced from which the offspring develops.

Like all cells, the sex cells contain the biochemical DNA. So when the sperm and egg cells fuse, the new cell has some DNA from the male and some from the female. As we have seen, DNA is the chemical that controls the building of new cells. The DNA from a human sperm cell may carry instructions that give rise to curly hair while the DNA from the mother may "program" eye color.

Farmers control the breeding of their livestock by mating together those adults with the most desirable characteristics. Friesian cows, for example, have been bred over the years to give large yields of milk. Similarly, different types of wheat have been developed that mature earlier and give bigger crops.

Doubling the DNA Code

The structure of the DNA in chromosomes enables them to copy themselves. Before a cell divides, the two strands of the DNA chain unwind. A new strand is built onto each side of the divided DNA, by pairing with free DNA units present in the cell nucleus. Because the DNA units only pair in particular ways, two exact copies of the original chromosome are made.

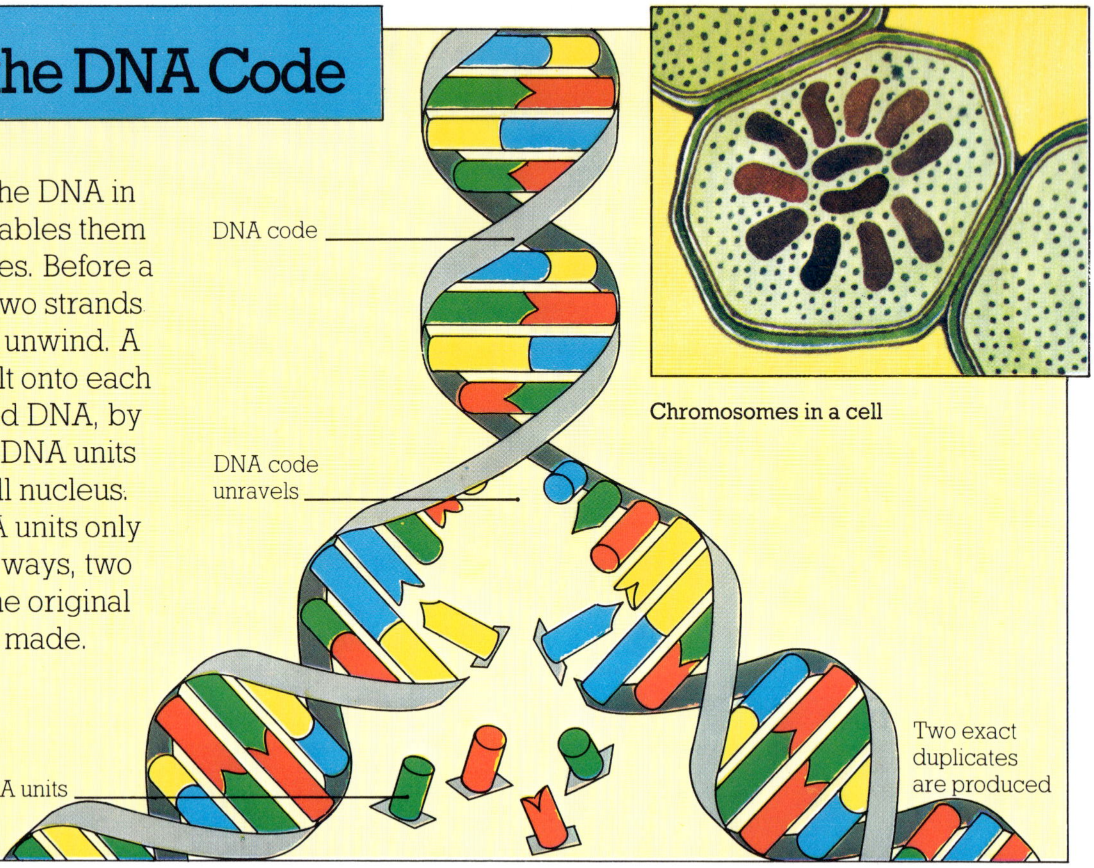

Chromosomes in a cell

Simple Cell Division

The fact that chromosomes can duplicate themselves is the key to growth and cell division. Just before cell division, the chromosomes thicken and can sometimes be seen under the microscope (1). The chromosomes then duplicate (2) and the nucleus of the cell begins to divide (3). When the division is complete (4), two identical cells are formed. In this way, new cells are produced for growth or to replace dead or damaged cells. Single-celled animals, and some plants, reproduce in this way. At the end of special stems on a spider plant, for example, cells divide and develop into a bud. This bud will grow into an adult plant identical to its parent.

A spider plant

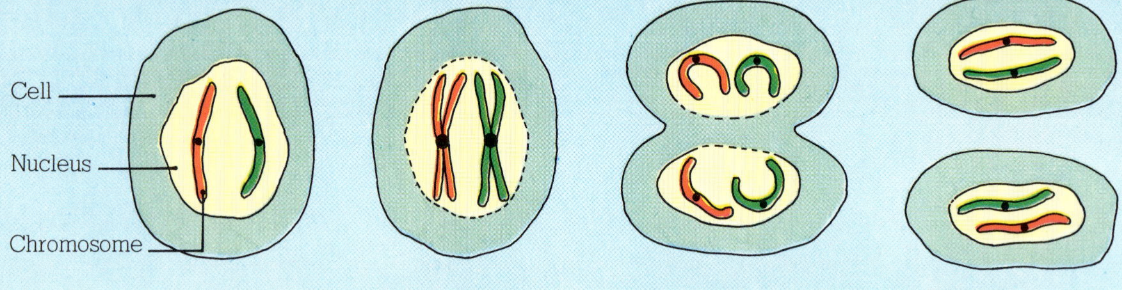

1 Cell prepares for division

2 Chromosome duplicate

3 Chromosomes and nuclei separate

4 Cell divides

Sexual Reproduction

Making sex cells

Sex cells are made by a special kind of cell division. As in ordinary cells, there are pairs of chromosomes (1). The chromosomes of each pair divide, giving four strands which stick together lengthwise, and then break and rejoin at various points (2). This allows groups of genes to be swopped between the chromosomes of a pair. The cell then divides in the normal fashion, creating two cells each with a pair of chromosomes (3). These cells divide again, creating four cells, each of which has only half the number of chromosomes of the original cell (4). Furthermore, each of these cells carries different chromosomes because of the genes being swopped at stage (2). This means that, after fertilization, they result in different offspring. Both sperm and egg cells are made in this way.

1 Cell prepares for division
2 Chromosomes double and intermix
3 First division complete
4 Sex cells produced by second division

A cat family

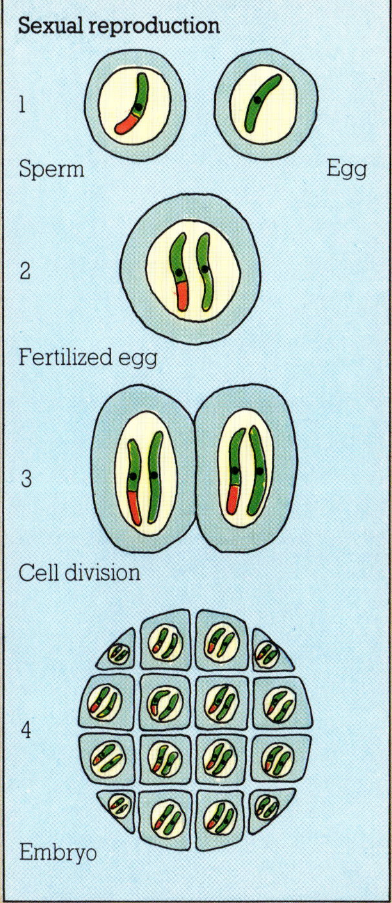

After fertilization

At fertilization, sperm and egg cells are brought together (1). The sperm cell fuses with the egg (2), creating a new cell which now has the full set of chromosomes – one half-set from the mother and one from the father. The fertilized egg then divides (3), eventually producing a group of cells called the embryo (4). The embryo then develops into the young animal, its growth controlled by the DNA it has inherited in its parents' chromosomes. Offspring of sexual reproduction always differ slightly from their parents – as you can see from any litter of kittens – because they inherit different combinations of chromosomes.

Evolution

All animals in the wild face a fierce struggle for survival. These zebras of the African grasslands are often short of food, as grass is killed by drought or eaten by other grazers. Predators such as lions and hyenas kill the weak and unwary, and diseases also take their toll. But because zebras reproduce sexually – and therefore have offspring that have inherited different characteristics from their parents – some will be better able to survive these hazards than others. One individual may have inherited a better resistance to disease, for example, while another may be stronger and better able to escape from predators.

Individuals best suited to survive will be more successful in mating than their less "fit" competitors, so their useful characteristics will be passed on to *their* offspring. In this way, over millions of years, a species will change to the changing conditions of its environment. This process of change is known as "evolution."

All of the different life forms found on Earth today are products of evolution. The way that species have changed can be discovered by fossil records – the remains of animals or plants found preserved in rocks that date back millions of years. Human beings and the great apes such as chimpanzees and gorillas are thought to have evolved from a common ancestor. Different individuals of this common ancestor began to adapt to their environment in different ways, one set gradually evolving to become gorillas, the other developing into our species – human beings. When evolution is traced back far enough, we find that all living things are related in some way.

▽ The hot, dry grasslands in parts of Africa contain many interesting species, especially mammals, adapted in different ways to their environment. Zebras and giraffes have both evolved striking coat patterns which make them difficult to see from a distance. This gives them protection from the animals which prey upon them.

Planning for survival

Young animals are particularly vulnerable to death from disease, predators and starvation. To overcome this problem, the zebra and other mammals have a few offspring which are born well-developed. The cod uses another plan. It sheds millions of eggs into the sea so that although most die, some survive.

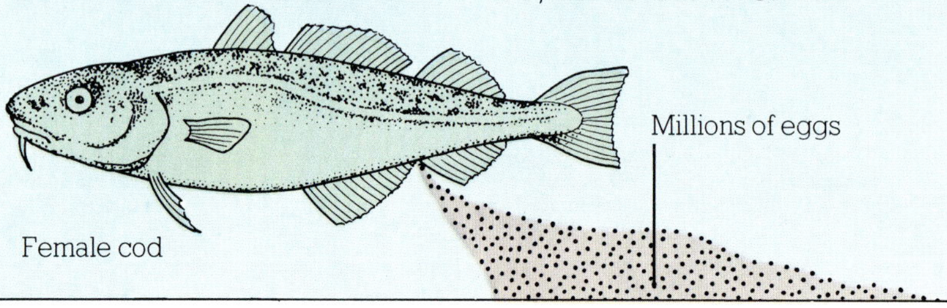

Adapting to change
Giraffes, with their long necks are well suited to feeding on the leaves of the Acacia tree. Their ancestors could only graze on short trees and bushes. As any individuals with longer necks could reach more food, they survived and bred more successfully. So gradually, through natural selection, the longer-necked modern giraffe developed.

Natural Selection in Action

Many animals are colored in such a way that they blend in with their surroundings. The yellow-brown fur of African lions camouflages them among the tropical grasslands in which they live, so that they will not be seen by their prey. These areas stay much the same all year so the lions are always camouflaged. The situation is quite different for animals such as these European banded snails.

A thrush breaking open a snail on a stone "anvil".

Banded snails have different shell patterns.

Different habitats

In the climate of northern Europe, these snails can live in places with very differently colored backgrounds, such as grassy meadows or dark woodlands. However, these snails have several distinct shell patterns. Each provides good camouflage for particular habitats. Thrushes kill and eat many snails, using favorite stones called "anvils" to break them open. By looking at the fragments of snail shell at a thrush anvil, it is easy to see that those most commonly eaten had the least protective shell pattern for their local surroundings, so fewer of that kind would survive to breed in that area.

Good camouflage in spring and summer grassland.

Good camouflage in late summer and fall grassland.

Good camouflage at the bottom of dark hedgerows.

Good camouflage in dead leaves of a wood.

Mutation

Mutation

Occasional mistakes may occur when DNA copies itself. These alter the DNA's chemical code by changing the order of units in a gene. Such an error, called a *mutation*, alters the protein assembled by the gene. This in turn may affect how an organism develops, so that it differs from normal, becoming a "mutant." This all-white or albino tiger is a mutant. As it has lost its normal fur color, it is badly camouflaged and so will be less successful in the struggle for survival.

An ordinary tiger

An albino tiger

When Does One Species Become Two?

By selective mating we have been able to create dogs as different as the spaniel and the dachshund. But these can still mate with each other and produce offspring, so they are still both of the same species. In the Galapagos Islands in the Pacific Ocean, there are two varieties of giant tortoise. A long-necked form on one island is adapted to feeding on cacti, while a short-necked variety on a different island feeds on grass. We can imagine that originally a single tortoise population lived on the islands. Over thousands of years, the two groups evolved differently as they adapted to changing conditions. In time, as they continue to evolve separately, these two varieties of tortoise may be unable to breed together and so will become separate species.

Varieties of dogs

Galapagos giant tortoises

Short-necked tortoise from Albermarle island.

Long-necked tortoise from Abingdon island.

Plants and Animals

We are familiar with the plants and animals that have evolved on land and find it easy to tell one from another. But life in the sea has evolved under very different conditions and has taken on many strange and beautiful forms. Nowhere is the variety of ocean life shown better than in the coral reefs found in tropical waters.

A coral reef is a dramatic underwater landscape of cliffs and canyons, covered with what appears to be a carpet of tiny flowers. Living on the reef are sea fans, sponges, spiny sea urchins, giant clams, starfish, worms and a host of brilliantly-colored fish.

The most abundant animal on the reef is the coral itself. Corals have a skeleton of limestone minerals from which the reef is formed. The "flowers" are the means by which the corals feed. These are tentacles containing tiny stinging cells which shoot out a hooked thread into their prey before drawing it back into the coral's mouth.

In fact, it is the method of feeding that distinguishes plants from animals. Animals must obtain their food from the dead or living bodies of other living things. All animals are hunters in that they must either search for their food or lure it to them. Plants, on the other hand, are able to manufacture their own food inside their cells. They take simple chemicals from the environment around them: in the case of ocean plants, from the seawater itself. Land plants draw the chemicals they need from the soil and from the atmosphere.

Animals and plants living together

Corals trap prey with their tentacles just as sea anemones do. They can also obtain nourishment from single-celled plants which live inside their body walls. The corals receive food and oxygen from these plants and in return they give the plants carbon dioxide. Both organisms help each other and so benefit from living together. This kind of relationship is called *symbiosis*.

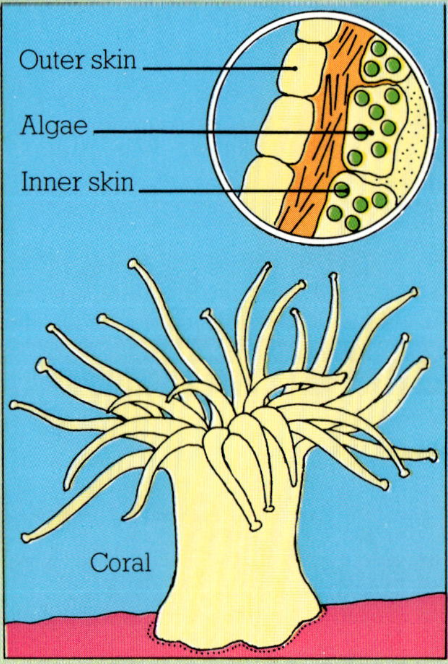

▽ Coral reefs are built up from the living skeletons of many kinds of marine organisms. Reefs can be hundreds of kilometers long and millions of years old. They shelter an astonishing variety of strange and beautiful life forms.

Key
Parrot fish
Staghorn coral
Trumpet fish
Four eyed butterfly fish
Sea whip coral
Pink anemone
Damsel fish
Seaweed
Red bearded sponges
Starfish
Banded anemone
Hepsitia fish
King coral
Spiny sea urchin

Plant Characteristics

Sea plants have very simple structures, because the water in which they live contains all the food chemicals they need. Land plants need to be more complicated to survive. They have roots which anchor them in the soil, and absorb water and the minerals which they need for growth. Their stems grow towards sunlight and conduct water and minerals to the leaves, where the plant's food is made. On land, wind and animals disperse the seeds produced by flowering plants away from their parents.

Sun
This provides the energy that green plants need to make their food.

Leaf
The green color in green leaves is caused by a chemical called chlorophyll, which absorbs the energy of sunlight.

Roots
These collect water and minerals from the soil for passage up to the rest of the plant.

Plant food

Green plants use sunlight to make sugar from carbon dioxide gas from the air and water. This process is called *photosynthesis*. The stems and leaves of many plants are green because they contain large amounts of a green substance called *chlorophyll*. This is found in the cells of the plant, where photosynthesis takes place. The chlorophyll absorbs energy from sunlight, and uses it to combine carbon dioxide with hydrogen from the water, to make a sugar called glucose. Oxygen is given off during this reaction. The sugar may be used to power other chemical reactions taking place in the plant's cells, or it may be stored in the stems, roots and leaves as starch for use later.

How plants make food

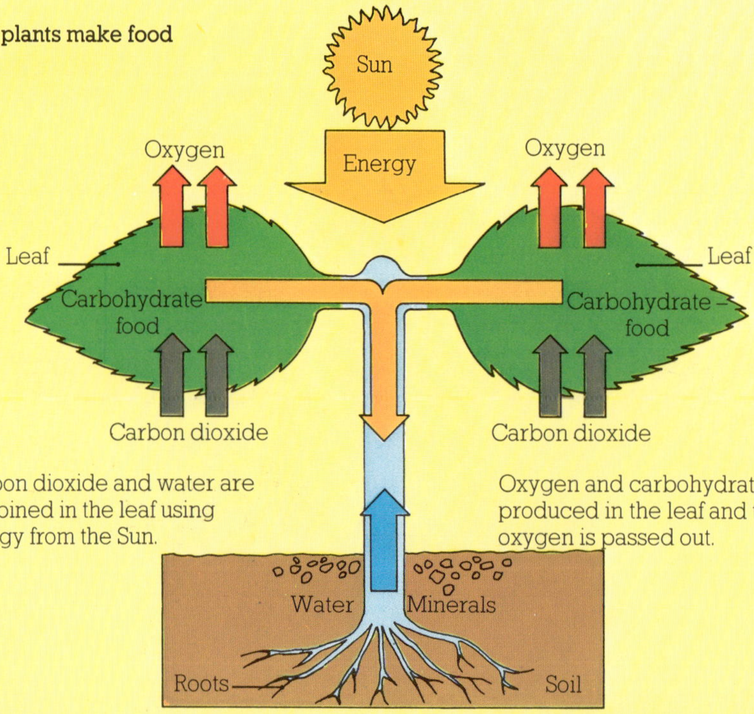

Carbon dioxide and water are combined in the leaf using energy from the Sun.

Oxygen and carbohydrate are produced in the leaf and the oxygen is passed out.

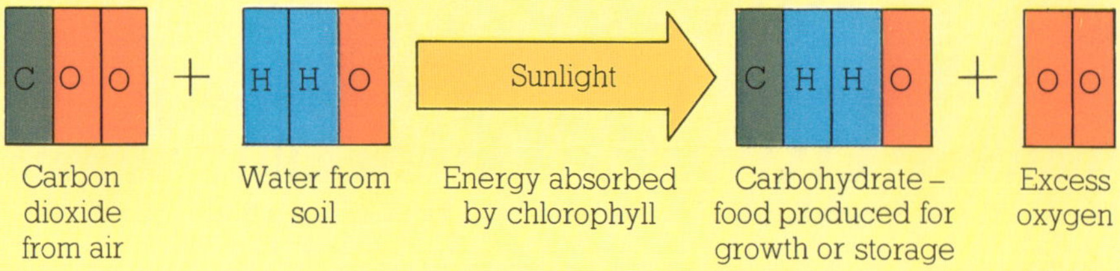

Animal Characteristics

Most animals actively move about. They need to find and eat their food, avoid dangers and search for a mate. Most animals move by using muscles. These are controlled by a network of nerves, connected to the brain. This, the body's "computer," is given information about the animal's surroundings by sense organs such as eyes and ears. Inside the brain are sets of instructions which control the body's behavior. Every movement of this cat's body, as it searches for the mouse, is controlled by instructions from its brain.

Animal food

Animals feed on plants and other animals. In the gut, food is broken down to simple chemicals which pass into the blood to reach all body cells. The cells take in food chemicals and use them for growth, or combine them with oxygen in a reaction called *respiration*. This releases energy needed for all the body's activities. Animals are specialists in particular ways of feeding. *Herbivores* – rabbits, for example – eat plants. *Carnivores* such as cats, are meat eaters, killing and eating other animals. Vultures are *scavengers*. They feed on dead animals. Bloodsucking ticks are *parasites* – they feed on another organism while it is still alive.

How animals release energy from food

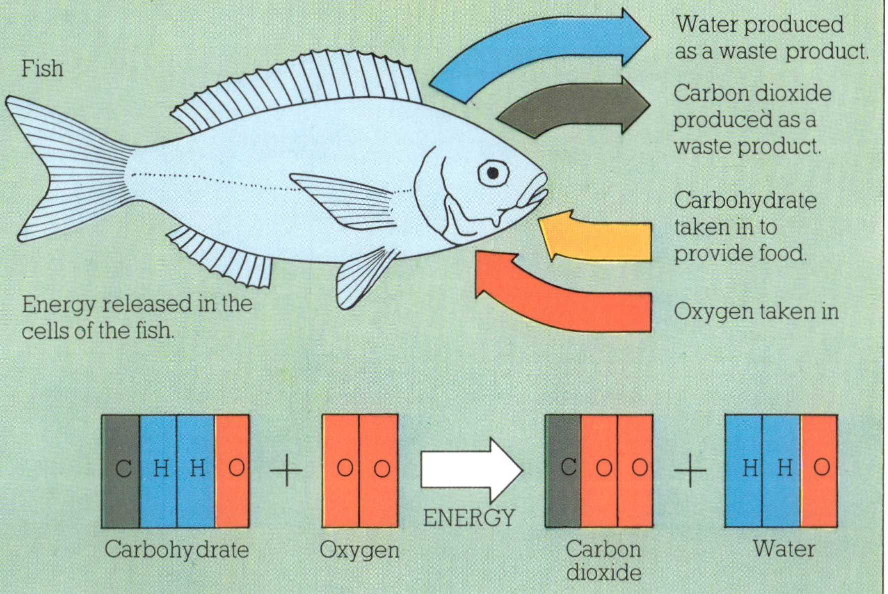

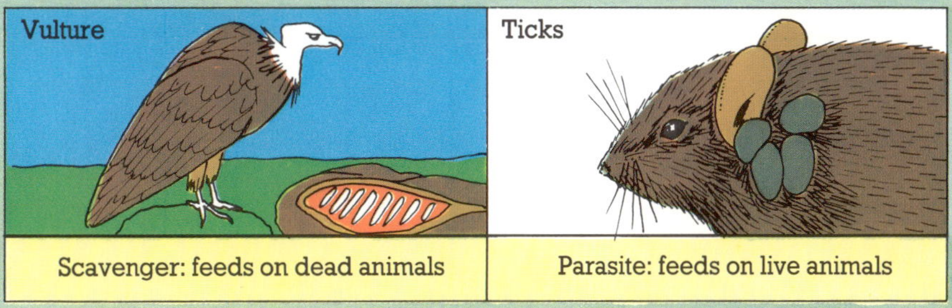

Microorganisms

How many living things are there in this kitchen? If you include the apples, perhaps a few dozen? Well, in fact there are billions of them. Almost all of them are microscopic organisms or "microbes." They are in even the cleanest of kitchens, in the air, on the surface of food, on our skin and inside our digestive systems.

Microbes occur everywhere on Earth, from the upper atmosphere to the seabed, and from buried rocks to scalding hot springs. Some of them, such as the single-celled animals found in pond water and the single-celled sea plants, we have met before. But there are three other great groups of microbes – the fungi, the bacteria and the viruses. Each group contains very many species.

When we make bread and wine, we use a familiar microscopic fungus called yeast. Lumps of yeast are simply vast numbers of yeast cells clumped together. Bacterial cells are even smaller than yeast cells. A thousand bacteria laid end to end would just stretch across a pinhead. Smaller still are the viruses, which are entirely parasitic and live inside plant, animal and bacterial cells.

Some microorganisms can cause serious diseases, but most are harmless and some actually help us. Bacteria and fungi are life's great garbage disposers. Microbes feed on wastes, breaking down or "decomposing" them. The carbon dioxide, water and simple chemicals which are produced by decomposition can be used by green plants. In this way the chemicals of life are endlessly recycled between plants, animals, microbes and the soil.

▷ Some microbes are welcome guests in the kitchen. Yeast is used in making bread and alcoholic drinks like wine, beer and cider. Certain bacteria that feed on lactose (a sugar in milk) are used to make cheese and yoghurt. Some molds are also used in cheesemaking.

Yeast
Yeast is a microscopic fungus which feeds on sugars, producing alcohol and carbon dioxide gas as wastes. When yeast feeds on or "ferments" grape juice, the gas escapes and the alcohol mixes with the juice, so producing wine. When yeast is mixed into bread dough, the gas is trapped in the mixture, making the dough expand or "rise."

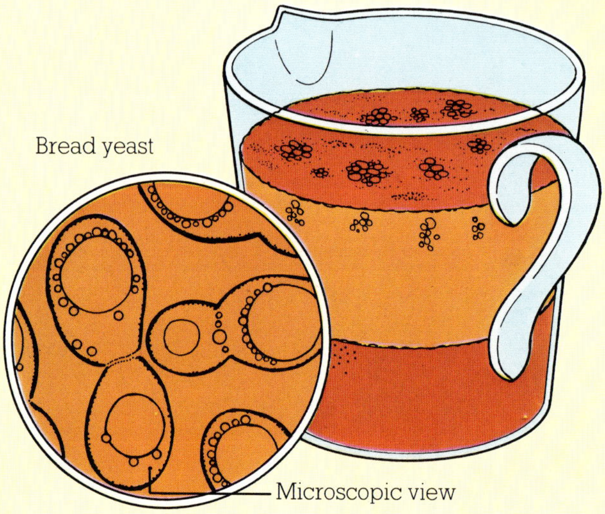

Viruses

Suffering from a cold

Viruses cause serious diseases like polio and smallpox, as well as minor ailments such as the common cold and warts. Viruses are so small as to be invisible under an ordinary microscope. They are the smallest particles with any of the characteristics of life. They lie on the borderline between living and non-living things. Even simpler in structure than bacterial cells, they consist mainly of a biochemical such as DNA surrounded by a shell of protein. Viruses can actually be made into tiny crystals just like a lifeless chemical.

A wart virus greatly magnified

When they penetrate a cell viruses take it over and reproduce themselves. Thousands of new viruses escape from the dying cell to infect other, healthy cells. Different types of viruses can infect plants, animals and even bacteria, but all are parasites.

Bacteria

Bacterial cells are much smaller and simpler than plant or animal cells. They are often cylindrical, spherical or even spiral in shape. Many bacteria move by beating whiplike "flagella" and they all have thick, protective cell walls. While a few bacterial species are harmful, causing human diseases such as tuberculosis, typhoid and pneumonia, many are essential to important natural processes. Without bacteria, grazing mammals, such as sheep and cows, would starve. In special chambers in their stomachs, billions of bacteria break down the normally indigestible cellulose of grass. The partly-digested grass is then returned to the mouth, chewed some more, and then digested normally. In the soil, other bacteria change nitrogen gas into chemicals which plants need for growth.

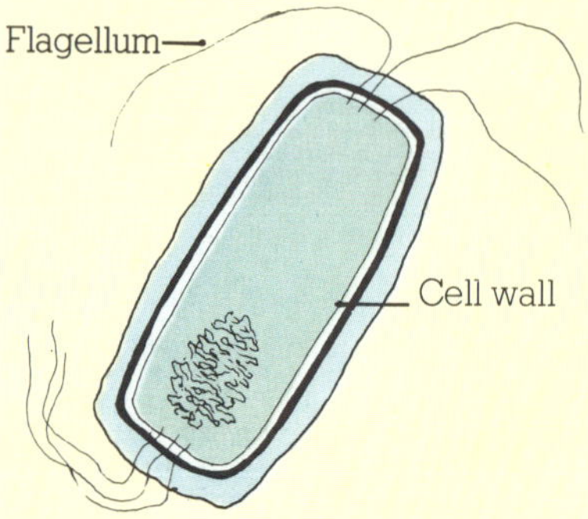

A typical bacteria

Sheep and cows

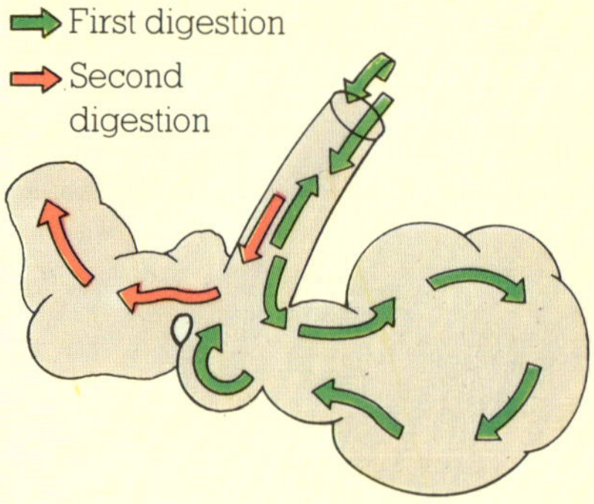

The stomach of a ruminant

Molds and Fungi

Structure of a fungus

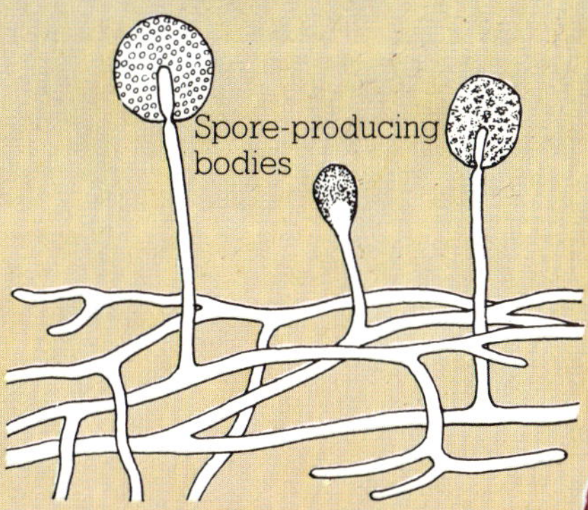

Fungi are larger than bacteria and have a more complicated structure. The single-celled yeasts are the simplest fungi. Other fungi, such as mushrooms, can be quite large. Fungi feed on dead or living plant and animal matter. They reproduce by producing tiny spores. These float in the air in huge numbers. If they land on suitable food, such as damp bread, the spores will start to grow. A network of fine tubes develops, growing through the bread, digesting and absorbing it. Spore-producing bodies are formed which release more spores to continue the fungi's lifecycle.

Moldy bread

Life in a Compost Heap

A garden compost heap

A compost heap uses the natural processes of decay that occur in the soil. Inside the heap, garden and household garbage is decomposed into its simpler chemical constituents, which will increase the fertility of the soil. Almost anything that has been alive can go on the heap, from potato peelings and lawn mowings to cotton rags. This material provides food for the plants and animals that colonize the heap from the soil below. The larger invaders include mice, earthworms, woodlice, insect mites, slugs and snails, but the accompanying army of microbes is by far the most important. The garbage slowly loses its shape and breaks apart as it is chewed and eaten by the larger animals, and tunneled into and attacked by both bacteria and fungi. The combined efforts of all these plants and animals eventually reduces all the garbage put onto the compost heap to a dark brown, powdery material called *humus*. When added to the soil, humus helps to bind it together and improves its texture. Humus is also an important natural fertilizer, giving back to the soil the simple chemicals needed for plant growth.

Living Communities

In living communities such as the oak forest shown here, or the coral reef and African grasslands we have seen earlier, each creature has evolved alongside all the others. The community exists in a delicate balance in which the particular needs of each species are met. Sometimes the relationship between two species is direct – predators obviously need the animals they prey on. In other cases, the link may be less obvious, but equally important for the survival of the community as a whole.

The study of the inter-relationships between the plants and animals in an environment is called "ecology." These relationships form a complex network involving the microorganisms in the soil, the plants that trap the energy of sunlight by photosynthesis and extract important minerals from the soil, and the insects and other animals. One way of unraveling the links in a community is to begin with the most dominant species in the environment and look at how other species depend upon it.

All organisms need food. We have seen that green plants make their own food from simple chemicals by photosynthesis. In any community the plants provide food for all the animals either directly or indirectly. The sequence of species which eat each other is called a *food chain*. Most food chains start with a green plant and end with a large meat eater. As one animal may be on the menu of several others, food chains are often cross-linked with one another to form *food webs*.

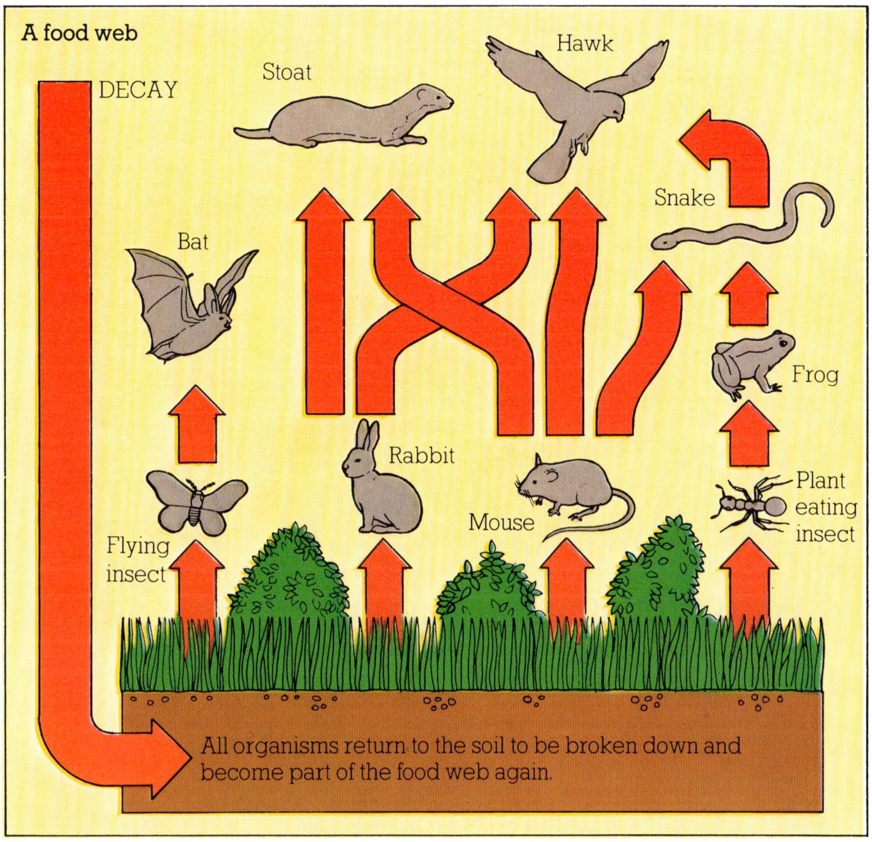

In this woodland, the oak is the dominant species. Its broad canopy of leaves traps energy for its own growth and reproduction and for the thousands of insects that feed off its leaves. Many of these are caterpillars and aphids that are preyed on by small carnivores such as spiders and ladybugs. These in turn are eaten by birds and small mammals. At the top of this food chain are the large carnivores such as stoats and foxes.

Each year, the oak sheds its leaves which fall to the forest floor to join the bodies of other dead plants and animals. This dead material provides the food for the huge armies of insects, molds and microbes that undertake the process of decay, returning important nutrients to the soil.

Where oak trees have been replaced by other species, as in a pine plantation, the community is drastically altered. Because pine needles do not decay as easily as oak leaves, the soil becomes less fertile and is able to support fewer plants. The great variety of insect life is lost and there are fewer species of birds. Within a few years, the ecology of the forest changes completely as the pines grow up and establish themselves.

Food Pyramids

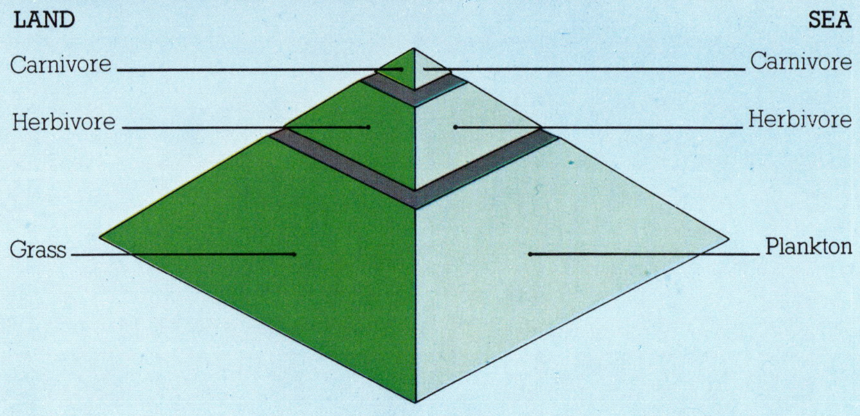

Whale feeding on krill

If all the organisms in a food web were to be piled up in a heap, they would form a huge "food pyramid." The bottom layer contains all the green plants. Above this would be a smaller layer of herbivores. On top of the pile would be one or two even smaller layers of carnivores. If each layer were to be weighed, we would find that the plant layer was the heaviest and the carnivore layer lightest. In the sea, microscopic plankton are eaten by tiny shrimp-like "krill," which are in turn eaten by whales. In this food chain, although the whales are very large, there are huge numbers of krill in the ocean weighing far more than all the whales put together.

The Flow of Energy

During photosynthesis, green plants trap the Sun's energy in the food they make. Some of the energy is passed on to plant eating herbivores. In the same way carnivores, when they eat herbivores, are taking in energy that once came from the Sun. As energy is used up in movement and growth, or lost to the air as heat, there is less energy available for animals further along the chain. And the larger an animal is, the more energy it needs. So as one link follows another, there are fewer animals in the chain, but they are often larger in size.

Lioness chasing antelope

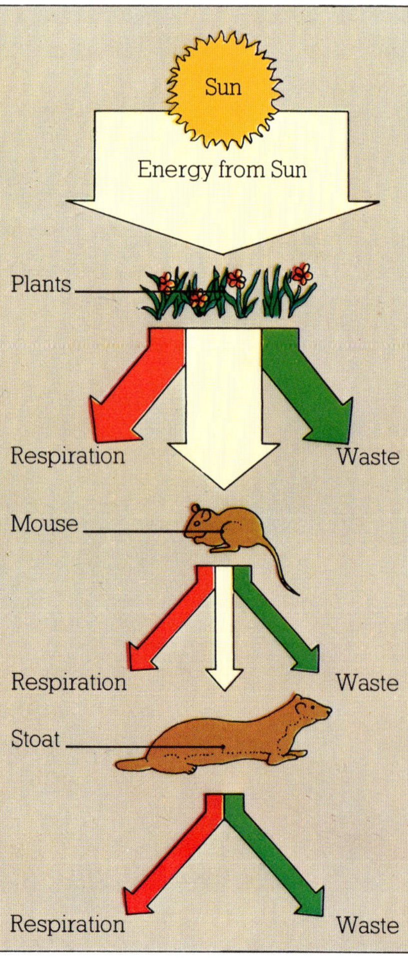

Natural Cycles

The carbon cycle

Carbon is found in all living things. Plants take in carbon dioxide from the air during photosynthesis and animals get their carbon from plants. If carbon were not returned to the air, there would eventually be no carbon dioxide left for the plants to use. In fact, carbon dioxide is returned directly each time animals breathe out, and it is also released when plants and animals decay. When things are burned, more carbon dioxide is given off.

In this way the carbon is endlessly recycled. Other chemicals have similar cycles. When you manure the garden, you are putting back nitrogen that is naturally recycled when plants and animals die and decay.

Succession

Waste ground or abandoned buildings do not stay barren for long. Soon they become a jungle of herbs and grasses as wind-carried seeds grow. If they are left undisturbed, young trees will begin to grow. Their leafy branches cut down the light falling on the plants below. Slowly the herbs and grasses become less dominant and the area develops into a natural woodland community. This process is known as *plant succession*.

Plants reclaim a site

Bacteria and fungi in the soil

A gram of fertile soil contains several million fungi and probably a hundred times as many bacteria. These microbes are important in breaking down dead organisms and waste matter. Soil microbes are used in making the antibiotics used to treat many diseases.

Glossary

Amino acids These are biochemicals (see below) that contain nitrogen. Proteins (see below) are made up of long chains of amino acids joined together.

Bacteria These are microscopic single-celled organisms. Some bacteria cause disease, but most are harmless or even helpful.

Biochemical Biochemicals are all those chemicals that are produced by living things.

Carnivore A carnivore is an animal that feeds on other animals.

Chlorophyll The green chemical pigment found in plant leaves which enables the plant to use the energy of sunlight to produce its own food by the process of photosynthesis (see below).

Chromosome Chromosomes are long strands of DNA (see below) found in the nuclei of all cells.

Digestion The process by which animals take in food and break it down into the chemicals they need to keep alive.

DNA DNA is the commonly-used abbreviation for *deoxyribonucleic acid*. It has a unique chemical structure which acts as a code, enabling it to direct the manufacture of proteins. DNA is the key to the way living things reproduce and pass on some of their characteristics to their offspring.

Gene A length of DNA containing the code to make one protein.

Herbivore An animal that feeds on plants.

Nucleotide Nucleotides are the basic chemical units from which DNA is made.

Nucleus The nucleus is found in all cells. It controls all the cell's activities and contains the cell's DNA.

Parasite A parasite is a plant or animal that feeds on other living things without necessarily killing them. A flea is an example of a parasite that feeds on animals.

Photosynthesis The process by which plants manufacture their own food from carbon dioxide and water, using the energy of sunlight which is absorbed by chlorophyll.

Phylum One of the large groupings used in the classification of living things.

Protein A complex biochemical made up of amino acids.

Species Plants and animals that have the same structure and are capable of breeding together. For example, all the people in the world belong to the species *Homo sapiens*, a Latin phrase which means "wise man."

Index

Natural Cycles

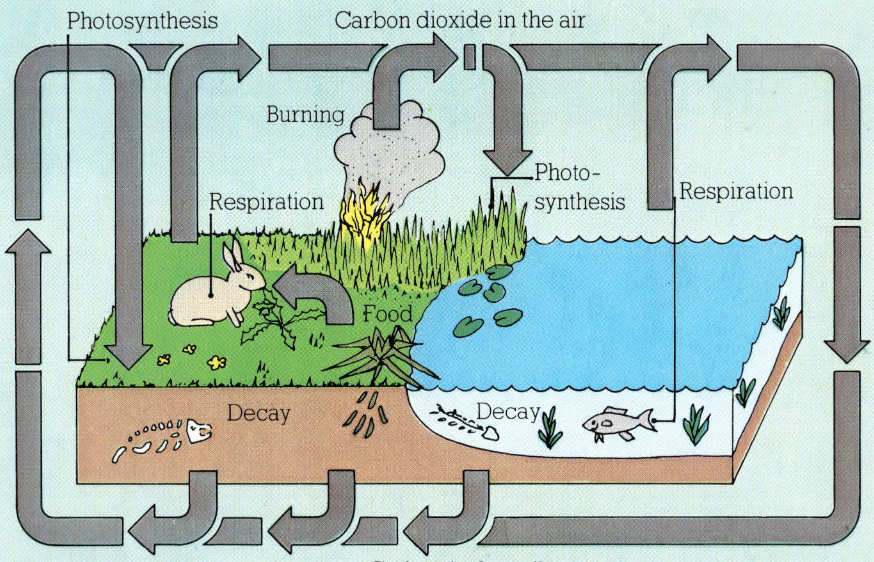

The carbon cycle

Carbon is found in all living things. Plants take in carbon dioxide from the air during photosynthesis and animals get their carbon from plants. If carbon were not returned to the air, there would eventually be no carbon dioxide left for the plants to use. In fact, carbon dioxide is returned directly each time animals breathe out, and it is also released when plants and animals decay. When things are burned, more carbon dioxide is given off.

In this way the carbon is endlessly recycled. Other chemicals have similar cycles. When you manure the garden, you are putting back nitrogen that is naturally recycled when plants and animals die and decay.

Succession

Waste ground or abandoned buildings do not stay barren for long. Soon they become a jungle of herbs and grasses as wind-carried seeds grow. If they are left undisturbed, young trees will begin to grow. Their leafy branches cut down the light falling on the plants below. Slowly the herbs and grasses become less dominant and the area develops into a natural woodland community. This process is known as *plant succession*.

Glossary

Amino acids These are biochemicals (see below) that contain nitrogen. Proteins (see below) are made up of long chains of amino acids joined together.

Bacteria These are microscopic single-celled organisms. Some bacteria cause disease, but most are harmless or even helpful.

Biochemical Biochemicals are all those chemicals that are produced by living things.

Carnivore A carnivore is an animal that feeds on other animals.

Chlorophyll The green chemical pigment found in plant leaves which enables the plant to use the energy of sunlight to produce its own food by the process of photosynthesis (see below).

Chromosome Chromosomes are long strands of DNA (see below) found in the nuclei of all cells.

Digestion The process by which animals take in food and break it down into the chemicals they need to keep alive.

DNA DNA is the commonly-used abbreviation for *deoxyribonucleic acid*. It has a unique chemical structure which acts as a code, enabling it to direct the manufacture of proteins. DNA is the key to the way living things reproduce and pass on some of their characteristics to their offspring.

Gene A length of DNA containing the code to make one protein.

Herbivore An animal that feeds on plants.

Nucleotide Nucleotides are the basic chemical units from which DNA is made.

Nucleus The nucleus is found in all cells. It controls all the cell's activities and contains the cell's DNA.

Parasite A parasite is a plant or animal that feeds on other living things without necessarily killing them. A flea is an example of a parasite that feeds on animals.

Photosynthesis The process by which plants manufacture their own food from carbon dioxide and water, using the energy of sunlight which is absorbed by chlorophyll.

Phylum One of the large groupings used in the classification of living things.

Protein A complex biochemical made up of amino acids.

Species Plants and animals that have the same structure and are capable of breeding together. For example, all the people in the world belong to the species *Homo sapiens*, a Latin phrase which means "wise man."

Index

PRINTED IN BELGIUM BY
proost
INTERNATIONAL BOOK PRODUCTION